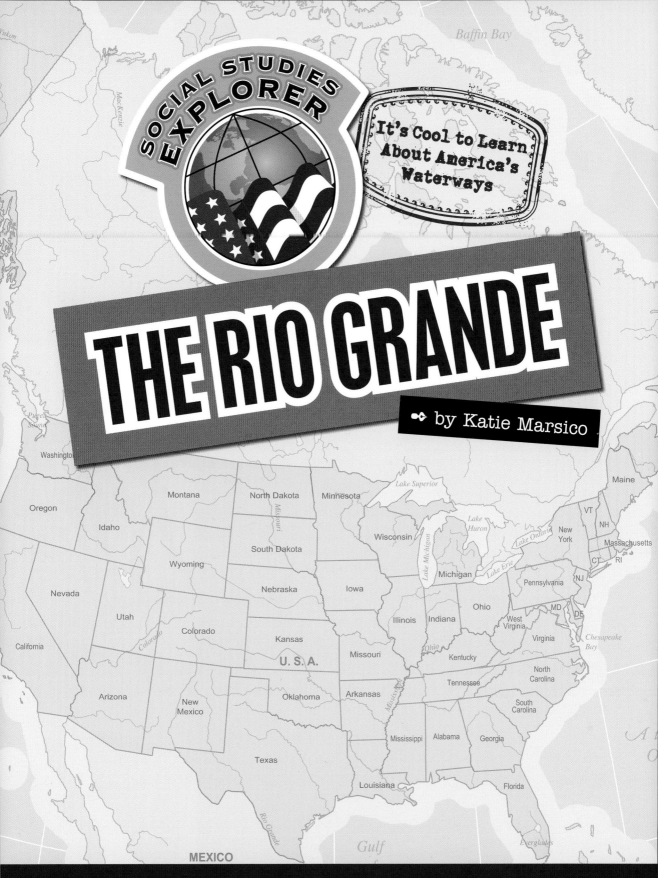

SOCIAL STUDIES EXPLORER

It's Cool to Learn About America's Waterways

THE RIO GRANDE

↔ by Katie Marsico

CHERRY LAKE PUBLISHING • ANN ARBOR, MICHIGAN

Published in the United States of America
by Cherry Lake Publishing
Ann Arbor, Michigan
www.cherrylakepublishing.com

Content Adviser: James Wolfinger, PhD, Associate Professor,
History and Teacher Education, DePaul University, Chicago, Illinois

Book Design: The Design Lab

Photo Credits: Cover and page 3, ©iStockphoto.com/mikenorton,
©Jeffbanke/Dreamstime.com, ©Centrill Media/Shutterstock.com,
©iStockphoto.com/yenwen, ©Neftali/Shutterstock.com; back cover and
page 3, ©photoBeard/Shutterstock.com; page 4, ©Jeffrey M. Frank/
Shutterstock.com; page 5, ©Peter Kunasz/Shutterstock.com; page 6,
©a. v. ley/Shutterstock.com; page 9, ©Mary Terriberry/Shutterstock.
com; page 10, ©Linda Armstrong/Shutterstock.com; page 11, ©Aurora
Photos/Alamy; page 12, ©Anton Foltin/Shutterstock.com; page 13,
©Michael Almond/Shutterstock.com; page 15, ©Paul S. Wolf/Shutterstock;
page 16, ©Chris Curtis/Shutterstock.com; page 18, ©MARKA/Alamy;
page 19, ©Val Armstrong/Dreamstime.com; page 20, ©Tom Baker/
Shutterstock; page 22, ©North Wind Picture Archives/Alamy; page
23, ©MSPhotographic/Shutterstock.com; page 26, ©Helen E. Grose/
Shutterstock.com; page 28, ©Roni Lias/Shutterstock.com.

Library of Congress Cataloging-in-Publication Data
Marsico, Katie, 1980–
    The Rio Grande / by Katie Marsico.
        p. cm. — (It's cool to learn about America's waterways)
    Includes bibliographical references and index.
    ISBN 978-1-62431-012-6 (lib. bdg.) — ISBN 978-1-62431-036-2 (pbk.)
— ISBN 978-1-62431-060-7 (e-book) 1. Rio Grande (Colo.-Mexico and
Tex.)—Juvenile literature. 2. Rio Grande Valley (Colo.-Mexico and Tex.)—
Juvenile literature. I. Title.
    F392.R5M376 2013
    978.8'3—dc23   2012035444

Cherry Lake Publishing would like to acknowledge the work
of The Partnership for 21st Century Skills. Please visit
www.21stcenturyskills.org for more information.

Printed in the United States of America
Corporate Graphics Inc.
January 2013
CLSP12

THE RIO GRANDE

TABLE OF CONTENTS

CHAPTER ONE

WELCOME TO THE RIO GRANDE!

➥ The Rio Grande is one of the longest rivers in North America.

Are you ready for an adventure on the Rio Grande? The words *rio grande* are Spanish for "great river"— a perfect name for the waterway you are about to explore! Your travels will mostly take place in the southwestern United States. On your journey, you'll see several unforgettable sights. An amazing variety of plants and animals live in or along the river. Prickly pear cactus, cats called ocelots, and Rio Grande silvery minnows are just a few examples. You'll also get to learn about Spanish explorers, Pueblo Indians, and local culture and **cuisine**. (If you've never tried Tex-Mex food before, prepare to sample some delicious meals!) Finally, when you leave the Rio Grande, you'll understand what *you* can do to help care for this national treasure.

Before you pack, however, you need to know a bit more about where you're headed. First, you should know that experts differ on the exact length of the Rio Grande. Some people say it stretches 1,800 miles (2,897 kilometers). Others argue that this measurement is actually closer to 1,900 miles (3,058 km). Depending on whom you listen to, the Rio Grande is either the fourth- or fifth-longest river in North America.

The Rio Grande begins as a stream in Colorado's San Juan Mountains. From there it flows south through New Mexico. The waterway then curves southeast and forms roughly two-thirds of the border between Texas and Mexico. It then empties into the Gulf of Mexico. From beginning to end, the Rio Grande passes through three U.S. states and four Mexican states.

The San Juan Mountains mark the starting point of the Rio Grande.

Be sure to get plenty of rest before your adventure. After all, you have lots of ground to cover! The Rio Grande's watershed includes almost 340,000 square miles (880,596 sq km) of land. A watershed, or basin, is the region drained by a river and all of its **tributaries**. Roughly half of the Rio Grande's watershed is located in the United States. The other half lies across the border in Mexico.

The six main tributaries that supply water to the Rio Grande are the Pecos, Chama, and Puerco Rivers in the United States; and the Conchos, Salado, and San Juan Rivers in Mexico. The Rio Grande is an extremely important river system in both the United States and Mexico. Because it is so large, however, you probably shouldn't try to check out the entire watershed in a single trip. So, from this point forward, let's limit your journey to those parts of the river that flow through Colorado, New Mexico, and Texas.

➽ The Chama River is one of many waterways that flow into the Rio Grande.

ACTIVITY

STOP
Don't write in
this book!

THE RIO
GRANDE

RIO GRANDE MAP

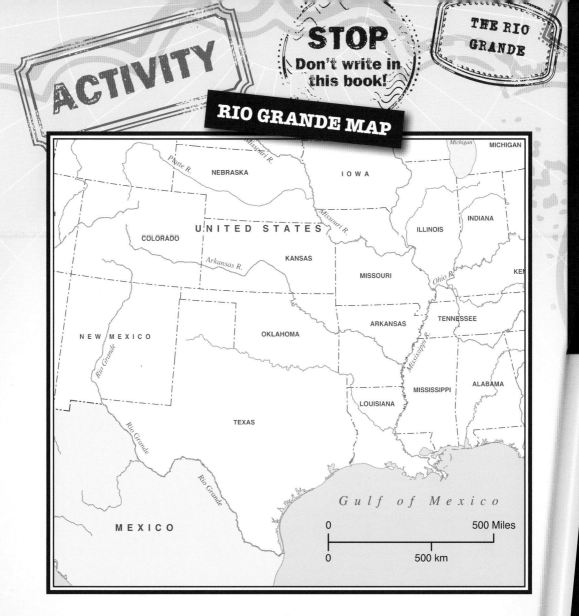

Take a close look at this map of the Rio Grande. Then lay a separate piece of paper over it and trace the waterway. Label Colorado, New Mexico, Texas, and Mexico. You might also want to identify the Gulf of Mexico. Add any other important locations you read about as you continue traveling!

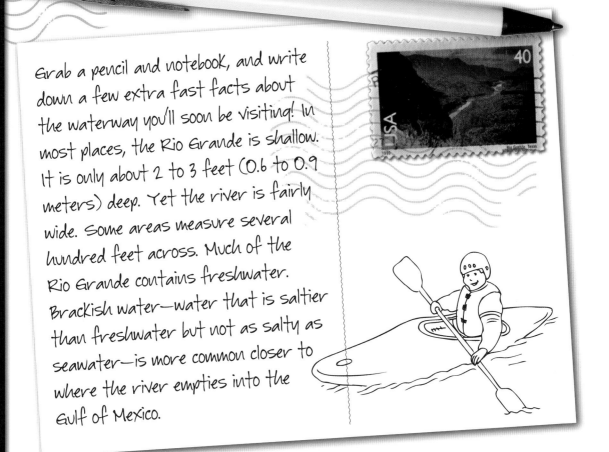

Grab a pencil and notebook, and write down a few extra fast facts about the waterway you'll soon be visiting! In most places, the Rio Grande is shallow. It is only about 2 to 3 feet (0.6 to 0.9 meters) deep. Yet the river is fairly wide. Some areas measure several hundred feet across. Much of the Rio Grande contains freshwater. Brackish water—water that is saltier than freshwater but not as salty as seawater—is more common closer to where the river empties into the Gulf of Mexico.

People often divide the Rio Grande basin into three main sections. The area between Colorado's San Juan Mountains and southwestern New Mexico is called the Upper Rio Grande. The Middle Rio Grande is south of this region and north of southwestern Texas. Finally, the Lower Rio Grande Valley stretches from Del Rio, Texas, to the Gulf of Mexico.

No matter which part of the Rio Grande basin you tour first, you should be ready to study a wide range of **habitats**. If you start in the Upper Rio Grande, you'll travel across mountain peaks and foothills filled with pine trees.

The Middle Rio Grande features marshes and grasslands. There are also bosques, or low-lying forests along the water. Once you arrive in the Lower Rio Grande Valley, you'll have the opportunity to explore a desert habitat. **Mesas** and **hot springs** are some of the interesting natural formations that shape the landscape there. When you get close to where the river empties into the Gulf of Mexico, you'll see shallow bays, salty lakes, and *lomas*, or mounds of wind-blown clay. Each of these environments plays a remarkable role in the waterway's **ecosystem**.

◆◆ Huge, flat mesas tower above the banks of the Rio Grande.

You should now begin to think about the local weather. Then you can decide how to pack for your adventure along the Rio Grande. The climate you'll experience depends on what part of the waterway you're visiting and when you plan to be there. Different parts of the Rio Grande watershed feature everything from blizzards and tropical storms to flash floods and **droughts**.

If you're going to be near the San Juan Mountains in January, make sure you take along a heavy coat—and possibly a pair of skis! This area receives an average of 38 feet (11.6 m) of snow a year. Temperatures often drop below freezing on winter nights. If you head to the southern Rio Grande basin in summer, however, you'll need to replace your

➥ The San Juan Mountains receive heavy snowfall in winter.

•◆ People in the Lower Valley sometimes wear long sleeves to avoid getting sunburned when spending a lot of time outside.

boots and scarf with sandals and sunscreen. Temperatures in Alamo, Texas in the Lower Rio Grande Valley have climbed to 106 degrees Fahrenheit (41 degrees Celsius) in August.

What about the water temperature of the river itself? Average temperatures in the Rio Grande range from near freezing in the San Juan Mountains to almost 91°F (33°C) farther south. But don't get too hung up on climate. You have to consider more than the weather when packing. So don't zipper your suitcase until you fill it with the equipment you'll need to do some serious wildlife watching!

CHAPTER TWO

THE WATERWAY'S WILDLIFE

➡ Wildflowers such as purple lupines fill the Rio Grande basin with beautiful colors.

You should bring a camera when you visit the Rio Grande. Or at least pack a sketch pad and some crayons! A picture is often the best way to capture the natural beauty along this waterway. In summer, the Upper Rio Grande sparkles with colorful wildflowers. You will see purple lupines and scarlet buglers. Trees such as ponderosa pines and Douglas firs also grow near the river in the San Juan Mountains. Willows and grasslike plants called sedges are found higher up in the mountain range. Sagebrush and other shrubs dot the foothills.

When you tour the Middle Rio Grande, be sure to snap a few photos of the cottonwoods. These trees tower up to 90 feet (27 m) above the bosques. There's a good chance you'll also spy prickly pear cactuses, coyote willows, and wolfberries. Be careful—the berries on this last plant may look red and juicy, but you should never eat them. They could be harmful to you.

Sunglasses will come in handy when you study plant species in the Lower Rio Grande Valley. How else do you plan to shade your eyes as you stare up at the region's sabal palmettos? The Lower Rio Grande Valley is also home to yucca plants—including the Spanish dagger—which have stiff, swordlike leaves. You might want to pack a pair of long pants to avoid getting poked!

➴ Watch out for the sharp, pointed ends of yucca leaves as you journey along the Rio Grande!

Binoculars are another item you should take along. You can use them to observe the many different animals living in and along the river. If you're traveling through the Upper Rio Grande, be on the lookout for American dippers. These songbirds are named for their ability to dip their heads underwater up to 60 times a minute. They do this to hunt for insects and fish eggs. Your binoculars will also help you spot elks—as well as any hungry black bears that might be roaming nearby! Bears and large hawks called ospreys often eat the Rio Grande cutthroat trout, which live in the river's northern waters.

Not all of the plants you'll see in the Rio Grande belong there! Hyacinths and hydrillas are examples of **invasive** species. This means that they were not part of the waterway's original ecosystem. In many cases, people either accidentally or purposely introduced invasive species to a certain area. Invasive water plants such as hyacinths and hydrillas clog the flow of the Rio Grande. They also reduce the river's oxygen levels, which harms the health and habitats of other local species of plants and fish.

◆◇ Roadrunners are among the many birds that live near the Rio Grande.

Look around for Rio Grande silvery minnows, Rio Grande bluntnose shiners, and shovelnose sturgeons farther south. These fish swim through the middle part of the waterway. Reptiles and **amphibians** found in this area include bull snakes, western painted turtles, and northern leopard frogs. Local birds range from Canada geese and great horned owls to bald eagles and roadrunners. You might also catch a glimpse of mammals such as mule deer, coyotes, beavers, bats, and muskrats.

→ Javelinas are also known as peccaries.

If you're super lucky, maybe you'll see a "ghost cat" in the Lower Rio Grande Valley. That's what some people call ocelots. These mysterious wildcats are spotted only at night. Sadly, scientists suspect that just a few dozen ocelots remain in the United States.

Ocelots share the Lower Rio Grande Valley with American alligators and piglike creatures called javelinas. Many birds nest along this section of the Rio Grande. These include brown pelicans, turkey vultures, trumpeter swans, and peregrine falcons. The river's southern waters are home to bass, carp, catfish, shad, and many other kinds of fish.

If you want the time to check out all of the waterway's wildlife, there's not a moment to lose. So, close up your suitcase and start your journey! (And make sure you're wearing a wristwatch. The first part of your adventure will involve a little bit of time traveling.)

Make Your Very Own Field Guide

It's smart to stay organized as you observe the Rio Grande's wide variety of wildlife. A field guide will help you keep track of all the plants and animals you're likely to find in and along the waterway. Luckily, you don't need to buy a field guide. You can create your own! Simply pick 20 species of local wildlife (or more if you want). Write the name of each one on a separate sheet of paper. Then get ready to do some detective work on a computer or at the library. Track down and record the following information for the plants and animals you have selected:

MATERIALS
- Type of plant/animal: (tree, shrub, flower/ reptile, mammal, fish)
- Habitat:
- Appearance:
- Other interesting facts:

After you're finished, either print out or draw pictures of the species featured in your field guide. Finally, decorate a cover and staple your pages together, or snap them into a binder. Be sure to pack your field guide before you visit the Rio Grande!

CHAPTER THREE

PAST AND PRESENT

Pretend for a few minutes that you're not touring the Rio Grande during the 21st century. Instead, you're visiting between 35 million and 29 million years ago! This is when pieces of the earth's outer layer started to stretch and spread apart where the river now exists. The result was a rift, or crack. This caused sunken areas to form in the earth's surface. Over time, these basins filled with water that developed into a steady flow. The flow eventually became the Rio Grande.

Researchers believe that early peoples began living along the waterway about 12,000 to 11,000 years ago. During the centuries, American Indian groups

⇨ Many Navajos still live in the southwestern United States.

such as the Pueblos, Apaches, and Navajos set up villages within the Rio Grande basin. In the 16th century, Europeans began to explore the river. Spain controlled the Rio Grande until the early 1800s, when Mexico declared its freedom from Spanish rule. In 1848, U.S. and Mexican leaders formally agreed that the waterway would serve as part of the border separating the two countries.

Today, the Rio Grande watershed stretches across portions of 66 counties in Colorado, New Mexico, and Texas. In 2000, roughly 3.6 million people lived in the American part of the Rio Grande watershed. Experts expect that number to grow to almost 6 million by 2030.

↦ Albuquerque, New Mexico, is one of the major cities located in the Rio Grande watershed.

Farming, manufacturing, transportation, and the production of energy are important businesses in the Rio Grande basin. Several U.S. military bases are located there. As you're about to see, tourism also makes up a large part of the local **economy**.

Now that you understand a bit more about the past and present of the Rio Grande, it's time to officially begin your adventure! Are you ready to enjoy the great outdoors? You'll have a great time boating, hiking, and camping in the Rio Grande National Forest in south-central Colorado. Be sure to check out Big Bend National Park in western Texas, too. You can do a little bird-watching and stargazing along the river there. On a clear night, you can see about 2,000 stars twinkling over the waters of the Rio Grande.

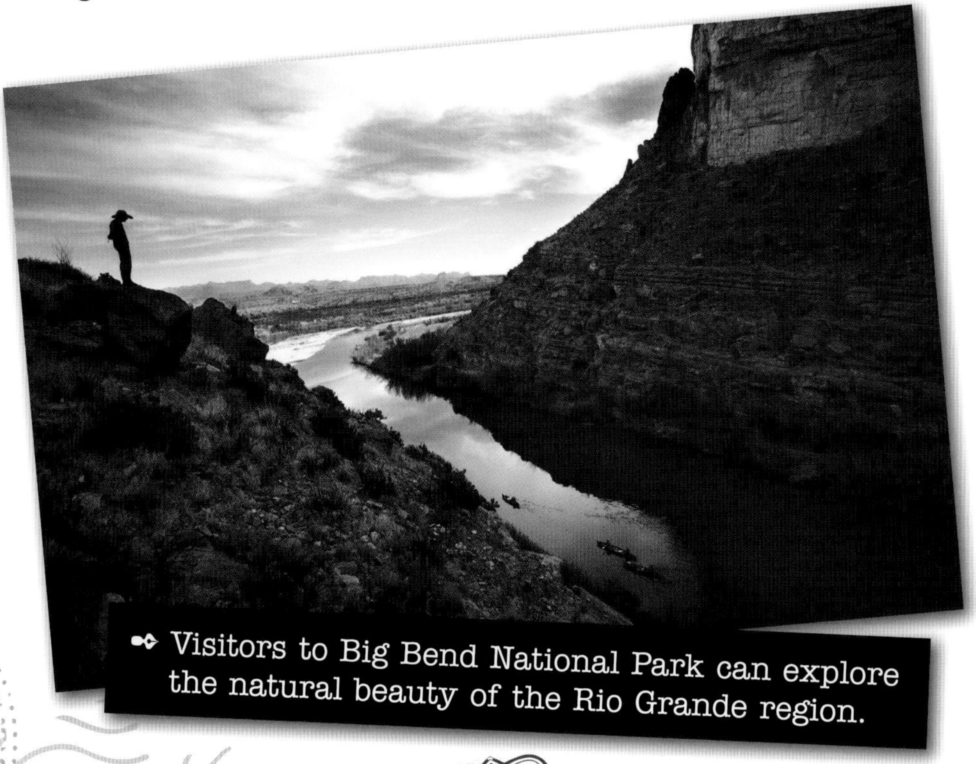

Visitors to Big Bend National Park can explore the natural beauty of the Rio Grande region.

ACTIVITY

TEST YOUR KNOWLEDGE

Are you an expert in U.S. history? Test your skills by completing this quiz on famous people who are connected to the Rio Grande. On the left side, you'll see the names of five individuals who are linked to the waterway. On the right side, you'll see the reasons these people earned their fame. Do your best to match each person with the correct description!

1) Francisco Vásquez de Coronado

A) U.S. explorer who located the source of the Rio Grande in Colorado (although he mistakenly believed it was the Red River!)

2) Popé

B) Mexican revolutionary leader who raided American border towns in the Lower Rio Grande Valley

3) Zebulon Pike

C) U.S. Secretary of Homeland Security (the official who oversees efforts to protect the country from outside threats) who grew up in the Rio Grande basin

4) Pancho Villa

D) Explorer who opened much of the U.S. Southwest to Spanish settlement and who was one of the first Europeans to cross the Rio Grande

5) Janet Napolitano

E) Pueblo religious leader who led a successful war against Spanish settlers and who helped his people briefly regain control of the Rio Grande basin

STOP
Don't write in this book!

Answers: 1) D; 2) E; 3) A; 4) B; 5) C

Between 1846 and 1848, the United States and Mexico fought an armed conflict known as the Mexican-American War. The main reason for the war was that each nation claimed Texas as part of its territory. The United States won the war. Both countries agreed to make the Rio Grande the border that separated their lands. During your adventure, try to stop at Brownsville, Texas. There you can explore historic battle sites located along the river.

Perhaps you're interested in finding out more about how American Indians have influenced the culture of the Rio Grande basin. Simply head to the Indian Pueblo Cultural Center in Albuquerque! This museum features traditional Native American dance performances. It also contains exhibits on Pueblo art, history, and food.

Have you been so busy sightseeing along the Rio Grande that you forgot to stop to eat? Drop what you're doing and dig into a Tex-Mex meal! This blend of Texan and Mexican cooking often includes ingredients such as melted cheese, meat, beans, and tortillas. Mexican tortillas are thin, flat pancakes made from cornmeal or flour. Chili, nachos, and fajitas are examples of popular Tex-Mex dishes. You'll find similar cuisine along the Rio Grande in New Mexico and Colorado. Make sure to keep a bottle of water handy. Many dishes are prepared with spicy, hot peppers called chilis, which are sure to wake up your taste buds!

Of course, you can't leave the Rio Grande without enjoying a tasty dessert! Before you go, sample some Pueblo bread pudding. You might also enjoy trying a slice of pumpkin pinyon sweetbread. This treat traces back to early American Indians who cooked using the seeds from small pine trees called pinyons.

◆ Chili is a spicy stew that usually contains tomatoes, beans, peppers, and some type of meat.

ACTIVITY RECIPE

You don't have to live in the Rio Grande basin to make a traditional Tex-Mex meal. In fact, you can pretend you're dining along the waterway when you wake up tomorrow morning! Try this breakfast recipe if you want a taste of the exciting foods and flavors that are part of Tex-Mex cuisine. Have an adult help you with any steps that involve slicing or dicing food, or operating a hot stove!

Tex-Mex Breakfast Tortillas

INGREDIENTS

2 large potatoes
2 large onions
2 large tomatoes
1 green pepper
1 pound turkey sausage
½ cup mild salsa

1 tablespoon hot sauce
½ teaspoon garlic powder
½ teaspoon salt
1 15-ounce can of chili
4 9-inch flour tortillas
½ cup shredded low-fat
    cheddar cheese

INSTRUCTIONS

1. Dice the potatoes, onions, tomatoes, and green pepper. Set these ingredients aside in a separate container for the moment.

2. Brown the turkey sausage in a skillet on the stovetop. Turn off the heat and allow the meat to cool for a few minutes before crumbling it into small pieces.

3. Turn the heat back on and stir in the chopped vegetables, salsa, hot sauce, garlic powder, and salt. Cook these ingredients in the skillet for about 20 minutes, or until the onions and green pepper seem tender. Remove the skillet from your stovetop so your Tex-Mex mixture can cool.

4. Warm the chili in a saucepan on the stovetop. Let it simmer, or slowly boil, for roughly 10 minutes. Then turn off the heat.

5. Fill each of the tortillas with about 1 cup of the Tex-Mex mixture. Then fold them up.

6. Spoon a little chili and shredded cheese onto the tortillas, and begin your day with a Rio Grande breakfast!

CHAPTER FOUR

TAKING CARE OF A NATIONAL TREASURE

↩ Ocelots face an uncertain future along the Rio Grande.

You probably hope to visit the Rio Grande again—but will it be the same when you return? It's difficult to say for sure, but most experts agree that the river is in serious trouble.

The Rio Grande is an important source of water. Yet overuse has decreased the river's water levels, and it sometimes dries up in places! Pollution and land development have destroyed a large number of local habitats. As a result, the Rio Grande is home to several threatened or **endangered** species. These include the Rio Grande silvery minnow and the ocelot. These species have a high risk of being completely wiped out.

ACTIVITY

GRAPHING WATER USAGE IN THE RIO GRANDE BASIN

Like many Americans living in the Rio Grande basin, people in western Texas depend on the river in a variety of ways. In 2010, residents used about 77 percent of the local water supply to **irrigate** crops. They directed roughly 20 percent of it to homes and businesses. About 3 percent of the local water was used to support activities such as manufacturing, mining, the production of energy, and the care of farm animals.

Review this information and create a bar graph illustrating water usage in western Texas. Can you predict which bar will be the longest? Which will be the shortest?

STOP Don't write in this book!

Fortunately, Americans everywhere can take steps to save the Rio Grande! Many people are encouraging **conservation** in and along the river. One example of their efforts involves paying careful attention to local water use. Conservationists are also studying dams and other structures that control the flow of the Rio Grande to see how they impact wildlife.

What can *you* do to care for the Rio Grande? Educate your community! Tell your family and friends about your exciting adventure along the Rio Grande. Explain why the "Great River" is truly a national treasure that Americans of all ages must guard and respect for years to come.

⊷ What other ways can you help protect the Rio Grande?

Government leaders in Colorado, New Mexico, and Texas are able to influence the future of the Rio Grande. Along with other politicians across the rest of the nation, they vote on laws and oversee projects that affect U.S. waterways. Writing a letter to these individuals makes them aware that people like you care about the Rio Grande. Ask an adult to help you find the addresses of officials who support conservation efforts in and along the river. Then create a short, simple letter using the following outline:

STOP
Don't write in this book!

Dear [INSERT THE NAME OF THE POLITICIAN(S) YOU DECIDE TO WRITE TO]:

I am writing to ask for your help in protecting the Rio Grande. The river is important to me because [INSERT TWO OR THREE REASONS THE RIVER MATTERS TO YOU]

Thanks for your efforts to support this amazing American waterway!

Sincerely,

[INSERT YOUR NAME]

GLOSSARY

amphibians (am-FIB-ee-uhnz) cold-blooded animals with a backbone that live in water and breathe with gills when young; as adults, they develop lungs and live on land

conservation (kahn-sur-VAY-shuhn) the protection of valuable things, especially wildlife, natural resources, forests, or artistic or historic objects

cuisine (kwi-ZEENZ) a style or manner of cooking or presenting food

droughts (DROUTZ) long periods without rain

economy (i-KAH-nuh-mee) the system of buying, selling, making things, and managing money in a place

ecosystem (EE-koh-sis-tuhm) all the livings things in a place and their relation to the environment

endangered (en-DAYN-jurd) at risk of dying out completely

habitats (HAB-uh-tats) places where an animal or a plant naturally lives

hot springs (HAHT SPRINGZ) sources of hot water that flow naturally from the ground

invasive (in-VAY-siv) tending to spread through and dominate a region where a thing is not native, such as plants and animals that have been brought into a region

irrigate (IR-uh-gate) to supply water to crops by artificial means, such as channels or pipes

mesas (MAY-suhz) large hills with steep sides and flat tops

tributaries (TRIB-yu-ter-eez) streams that flow into a larger stream, river, or lake

FOR MORE INFORMATION

BOOKS

Cunningham, Kevin, and Peter Benoit. *The Pueblo*. New York: Children's Press, 2011.

Tieck, Sarah. *Texas*. Minneapolis: ABDO Publishing Company, 2013.

WEB SITES

Indian Pueblo Cultural Center
www.indianpueblo.org
Find out about the history, language, and feasts of Pueblo peoples and watch videos that take a deeper look at their culture.

National Park Service—Rio Grande
www.nps.gov/rigr/index.htm
Learn more about the history, culture, wildlife, and science of the Rio Grande region on this U.S. National Park Service site.

The New Mexico Museum of Natural History and Science
www.nmnaturalhistory.org/BEG/BEG_Plant&AnimalCards_Home.html
This Web site includes detailed descriptions of different plants and animals living in the Middle Rio Grande basin.

INDEX

ABOUT THE AUTHOR
Katie Marsico has written more than 100 books for young readers. She has never visited the Rio Grande but would love to one day explore it with her husband and children.